LeBron James

------- ❧❦❧ -------

The incredible story of LeBron James – one of basketball's greatest players!

Table of Contents

Introduction

Thank you for taking the time to pick up this book all about NBA superstar LeBron James!

This book covers the story of LeBron and his incredible journey to the NBA. You will soon discover how LeBron was able to rise from humble beginnings, to achieve NBA championship success.

In detail, this book shares LeBron's experiences playing High School basketball, his first NBA seasons with Cleveland, his time playing in the Olympics, his stint in Miami, and finally, his most recent success back playing for the Cavaliers.

At the completion of this book you will have a good understanding of LeBron and his inspiring story, as well as what's next for the NBA champion!

LeBron's incredible story is one that we can all take inspiration and learn from. He has overcome many challenges throughout his life, while being publicly scrutinized most of the time. He's an incredible man to watch perform on the court, and is even more admirable when you know the details of his life and career that this book shares.

Once again, thanks for taking the time to read this book, I hope you find it to be enjoyable and insightful!

Chapter 1:

Early Life

LeBron James makes basketball look easy. He towers above other players, he sees the game like a clairvoyant, and his skill elevates the players around him. It's easy to imagine that the court is shorter, the rim lower, and the basketball is smaller when we watch LeBron play. But life wasn't easy for LeBron growing up in Akron Ohio. LeBron Raymone James was born to Gloria Marie James on December 30th of 1984. Gloria Marie James, only 16 at the time of LeBron's birth, was a single mother without a consistent job. She had to fight to provide for little LeBron, moving from job to job, apartment to apartment, scraping to make a living. It's easy to imagine LeBron watching his mother during this time in their lives, learning the true meaning of hard work and sacrifice, learning the value of time and energy spent working and with family. Gloria Marie James had to make the ultimate sacrifice for her son LeBron when he was only 9 years old. She realized she couldn't provide the kind of stable, consistent life for her young boy, and she decided to let him live with a community leader named Frank Walker. In retrospect, there are many decisions and paths that lead to greatness, and this moment certainly qualifies. Frank Walker was also a football coach for young kids, and believed in the power of sport to lift children up from their circumstances. Youth sports could teach important skills, and motivate kids to reach beyond what they had experienced so far.

It was Frank Walker that introduced a young LeBron James to the sport of basketball. The rise to prominence happened fast. LeBron took to basketball quickly, and the community began to take notice when he played for an Amateur Athletic Union Basketball team based out of Akron. The Amateur Athletic Union is a national amateur sporting organization, which provides access to children all over the United States to the sports that challenge and improve their lives. It was on this team that LeBron began to find his passion and talent for basketball. We can only wonder what would have happened if LeBron's young life had followed a different path. What if Gloria had decided to maintain LeBron in her home? Would he have found basketball in such huge strides? Would he have had time to focus on the sport at such a young age? Was it serendipity that landed LeBron in the home of a youth coach, so dedicated to using sport as a tool to empower children?

This was also a time when LeBron began to find a groove playing with a strong team. This basketball team, led by LeBron and some of his childhood friends went on to win many games locally in Akron, as well as around the United States. LeBron and his three friends called themselves "The Fab Four," and it was their combined talent and chemistry that made them so formidable playing around the United States. This is a unique experience for a young, talented athlete, to be surrounded by compelling players with their own momentous talent. A young LeBron was learning to appreciate the power of a tightly knit team. Only in middle school, the people of Akron were anxious to see which of the area high schools LeBron and his friends would choose. This would certainly determine much of the fate for High School basketball over the next four years. It was also a miniature introduction to the kind of fame and attention the young man was about to receive.

Chapter 2:

High School Career

LeBron James and his friends surprised the community by choosing St. Vincent-St. Mary Catholic High School, a college preparatory (and predominately white) private school. As an early teen, LeBron was already commanding attention from the local basketball community. His decisions were rippling outward, causing discussion and in some cases stirring conflict. The decision of the Fab Four to attend a white private school elucidated questions about their intentions and their commitment to their own communities.

But LeBron's High School game began to speak for itself almost immediately. Many High School players take a few years to build their game to the Varsity, or highest, level. These schools are usually able to field several teams across the age spectrum, often introducing players at the Freshman-Sophomore level to the more competitive elements of High School basketball by playing with other Freshmen and Sophomores. It isn't until Junior or Senior year that many players mature their game and their mentalities enough to contribute to the Varsity or Junior Varsity levels.

LeBron proved to be an exception.

Chapter 2: High School Career

In his freshman year at St. Vincent-St. Mary, he was already playing like someone who had led the team for years. He was scoring 25 or more points per game, which, for context, is often about one quarter of the entire team's points in that game. Think about that! A freshman player on the Varsity team contributing that much to the team's success. That success came often, too. The St. Vincent-St. Mary's team finished undefeated LeBron's freshman year, winning all 27 of their games and securing the league championship.

News traveled fast around Akron about this young player propelling his team to a clean sweep of their season's opponents. By LeBron James' sophomore year in High School, the team had to play several home games at the University of Akron just to allow more spectators an opportunity to watch the young boy play basketball. Attention like this can be a curse to a young player. How often does such a young talent, in the face of overwhelming assumptions for his or her future greatness, actually aspire to achieve or exceed those expectations? LeBron James, from the very outset of his career, was expected to be great. Not just great, the best.

In LeBron's first two years of High School, he was averaging between 21 and 25 points per game. He had won a Division III championship. The team was now moving up to Division II, and the eyes of the basketball scouting nation had already begun to look toward him.

Can you remember the last time you saw a High School player on the cover of Sports Illustrated? LeBron James was on the cover before he even started his Junior year. The scouting community was already referring to him as the number one recruit, the best High School basketball player in the country.

Many states give out a "Mr. Basketball" award to the best player in the state, which LeBron was named three years in a row, from his Sophomore year to his Senior year. Following each season, USA Today would produce "All-USA" basketball teams, as a measure of fielding the best players from around the United States. Being named to these teams is a huge honor for a young player, and LeBron was named to the team for three consecutive years, just like he was named Mr. Basketball.

Again, try to put yourself in the (particularly large) shoes of a young star athlete, like LeBron James at this age. He's been the focal point of attention since he was only 9 years old. Adults from all around his life are heaping praise and larger expectations onto him. Imagine the weight of those expectation as they begin to pile higher and higher. Now imagine that as an underclassman in High School, you're starting to appear on magazine covers that you read. The eyes of the entire nation are on you, all the time. Reporters and scouts from around the United States are starting to heap even greater expectations on you, all while you're just coming of age as a young man.

One of the true marks of greatness that you'll notice with LeBron James is his ability to deflect the negative effects of this kind of attention, in order to simply do what he does best - play great basketball. For many young players, these kinds of expectations would result in a disastrous implosion, and a rebellious rejection of the world's assumptions. But for LeBron, they felt natural, since they had been a part of his life for years.

As a Junior and Senior at St. Vincent-St. Mary's, LeBron continued to outperform the now massive expectations that he had been saddled with. He led the team to the new Division II championship, unfortunately ending in a loss. He was named Gatorade's National Player of the Year.

LeBron James even decided at this point that he was interested in heading directly to the NBA, rather than attend college. This is often a difficult decision for young players, who are weighing a college education (often paid in full by a scholarship), the promise of some kind of college experience, a potential National Championship, with the grandeur of the Professional playing experience. This conundrum plagues many young talented players, who do not want to squander a chance to either play professionally or obtain a college education. For LeBron, as the most talented High School player in the nation, there was apparently very little hesitation.

After this tough championship loss in the more difficult Division II game, LeBron declared that he was ready to enter the NBA. At the time, that was impossible because the NBA required at least a High School diploma to be eligible. LeBron petitioned unsuccessfully for the NBA to waive that requirement so he could be eligible for the draft.

LeBron James didn't petition the NBA to become eligible because it was his only option. It's important to understand that LeBron James was a lover of routines. Some biographers look back at his early childhood with Gloria, and they find a young boy who was desperate to have the kind of consistency and stability associated with a routine. When he moved in with Frank Walker, and when he found the private school routine at St. Vincent-St. Mary's, he found his routine. LeBron was always practicing, always doing his homework, he was a good student. It was just his dream to play in the NBA, to escape the prophesying and begin his career as a professional outside of all the anticipatory hype.

In LeBron's last year of High School, he had a season that most players would only ever dream of. His average of 31 points was unheard of. The team was so talked about nationally that they went on a tour to play the other nationally ranked High School teams, some of the games were even nationally televised. When was the last time you remember a High School basketball game being made available on Pay-Per-View? This kind of attention wasn't always good for LeBron James. There are quite a few laws and procedures that regulate amateur players, limiting their ability to accept corporate sponsorship in the form of gifts and compensation. LeBron James was suspended from being able to play High School basketball his senior year for accepting high valued gifts in exchange for providing his likeness to a sporting goods company, the definition of a sponsorship. He was suspended, but appealed and brought his penalty down to only two games missed from his senior year.

Following his senior year, LeBron James was a regular feature in several High School All Star games, including the McDonald's All American Game. The McDonald's All American game is a collection of the best boys and girls basketball athletes from around the US and Canada, and interestingly, most National Championship teams feature at least one participant from a past McDonald's All American Game.

It's also worth noting that LeBron James' athletic prowess wasn't limited to one game. He was a star player on the St. Vincent-St. Mary's football team, as a wide receiver he even achieved some acclaim. He was even recruited by several major collegiate organizations, like the Notre Dame Fighting Irish Football team.

Chapter 2: High School Career

It was clear where LeBron James was heading: the NBA. He was easily the most talked about High School prospect in his class, and arguably the most talked about High School player to date. His future was in the stars, he had handled an insane amount of pressure as a young man, and he was ready for all of it.

Chapter 3:

Headed to the NBA

The stage of any professional sport is a massive one. Millions of people from around the world follow their favorite team through the season and the offseason. Players' lives are followed closely by media outlets of every size, tenaciously scrutinizing each decision, each game, each move. As a person, you are suddenly elevated to the level of idol for generations of players and fans. As such, the expectations balloon ever outward from the second you sign your name to your first contract.

For LeBron James from Akron Ohio, this was his destiny. From the time he was 9 years old, coaches and teammates were whispering those three towering consonants, "N...B...A..." The time was finally here, he could push past the High School hype and begin to operate within the walls of his true purpose. The unsurpassed hype of LeBron James' career up to this point by all accounts should have been too much for any one player to amount to, but heading into the 2003 NBA Rookie Draft, maybe the hype prepared him for what was to come. Maybe he was the only player truly prepared for the media circus that was to become their lives. He had lived under the microscope for over a decade, and now there were just a few more people in the room to watch.

Chapter 3: Headed to the NBA

The "people" in that room were special. The 2003 NBA Rookie Draft was like a gold mine, a jackpot of talent. Carmelo Anthony, Dwayne Wade, and Chris Bosh all sat anxiously around the room in Madison Square Garden that night late in June, 2003. The Rookie Draft in the NBA is a lottery, meaning there is a higher percentage chance that the teams finishing lower in the previous year's standings will get the first pick for the next season. The Cleveland Cavaliers, favorites to win the first choice of Rookie talent in 2003, were fortunate enough to recruit LeBron James with the first overall pick.

The players chosen in this special environment would go on to become some of the greatest players in modern basketball, some of whom LeBron would have a chance to play with. As LeBron Raymone James stepped to the front of the room, few people were surprised. Scouts, commentators and industry columns had predicted this moment for years. They knew that the first pick would go to Lebron James. They knew they would see his smiling face holding that first jersey, just months out of High School. When many of his classmates were anxious about going off to school, starting the next phase of their lives, LeBron James stood in front of the cameras, yet again, ready to show the world what he could do next.

Chapter 4:

The First Season

Imagine a young, early teen LeBron heading to High School at St. Vincent-St. Mary's. He's left the first team he excelled at, he's entering a brand new arena of competition, and it's intense. The kids around him aren't sure they'll make the team. The kids who do make the team are anxious about a starting spot, getting playing time, scoring points, and looking good to their parents and the girls in the crowd. For LeBron James, these are the symptoms of what he does best. These are the things that come as a result of his hard work and preparation, on and off the court. He breathes basketball, he sees it differently, more intimately, than everyone else. When he plays, everything else happens around him, as a result of him.

LeBron James took to the professional stage in much the same way. The NBA is a collection of the greatest players from around the world, not just the best players from around Akron, or the Midwest. These athletes can do things most kids in Ohio will only dream of, while they watch on TV. Many of the athletes LeBron James is suiting up with aren't just two or three years older, some have been playing basketball since before he was born. For a kid coming straight from High School, this is like the World's Varsity team.

Chapter 4: The First Season

For many reasons, then, it's normal for a rookie High School graduate to struggle entering the NBA. It takes time, just like it takes time as an undergraduate, to acclimate to the new styles of play, the new class of athleticism, the public stage and the coaching.

It took LeBron James about five minutes to acclimate.

LeBron took the court against the Sacramento Kings in his first ever NBA performance on October 29th, 2003. In 42 minutes of playing time (basketball games are 48 minutes total), LeBron James scored an NBA record 25 points as a player fresh out of High School.

In that first season, LeBron James again stepped up to meet every ounce of hype that had been heaped onto him. In the completely new world of the National Basketball Association, LeBron still managed to average over 20 points, over 5 rebounds, and almost 6 assists per game. For that achievement, and for lifting the Cleveland Cavaliers up 18 games over their previous season's record, LeBron James was awarded the 2003-2004 Rookie of the Year.

The importance of this debut season in the NBA cannot be overstated. For a decade, since LeBron James was 9 years old, his supporters and critics had pointed to this moment. They had attested that surely he would make it to the NBA, and that his fate would hang on his ability to survive the highest level of basketball on earth. Now, nearly 20 years old, LeBron James had shown the world what was to come. He had proven that he could play at the highest level, and excel. He had demonstrated over the entire season that he would be one of the game's greatest players, and that no amount of media hype could prove otherwise. The name "LeBron James" had moved out of the scouting and industry circles, and into homes all around the world. He was free of the expectations, and now he could do what he did best: play basketball.

LeBron James even was invited to play basketball following this first season for the United States. 2004 was his first appearance on the US National Team as they played in Greece. LeBron played only a small role in the team's earning of a bronze medal from these games. As if playing in the NBA, and playing for his country wasn't enough to do during 2004, LeBron James also welcomed his first son into the world, LeBron James Jr. He had LeBron Jr. with his long time girlfriend and high school sweetheart, Savannah Brinson.

Then, it was time for LeBron James to return to the Cleveland team he was just beginning to thrive on.

Chapter 5:

Playoff Debuts

fter his first NBA season, LeBron James finally had
room to grow. He had been driving so hard to prove his
worth to the world of basketball and achieve status as a
professional player up until then, that now he could focus on
his game and becoming part of a championship team.

Over the next three seasons, the world watched as LeBron
James began to demonstrate the depths of his talent. In the
2004-2005 season, LeBron James grew his points per game
average to 27.2 points, up from 20 points his Rookie Season.
He was starting to find his groove, he was learning the
strengths and weaknesses of his teammates, and he was
starting to realize what he was capable of. LeBron set a
Cleveland Cavaliers single game scoring record with 56 points.
56 points in a single game! The world was shocked. He was the
youngest player to ever score more than 50 points in a single
game. For one player, guarded closely by the opposing team, to
be able to score over 50 points per game is astounding. 56
would not be LeBron James personal best, however. He was
just getting started.

With their young talent, the Cleveland Cavaliers were
improving year after year, albeit slowly. The city of Cleveland
could feel something special was happening though, as LeBron

James was awarded entry into his first NBA All Star Game, the likes of which he would become a staple of over the years. But, unlike in High School, the presence of LeBron James wasn't enough to elevate the Cavaliers directly to undefeated seasons and a championship. Those dreams would have to wait, as for the second year LeBron and Cleveland missed the playoffs.

It wasn't until 2005-2006 that the LeBron James had his first NBA Playoff experience, which was the first time the Cleveland Cavaliers had reached the Playoffs since 1998. This season is when LeBron James began to grow into the huge superstar he his today, as the league started to recognize the impact the young player was having. Although Cleveland was knocked out of the Playoffs in the second round, LeBron showcased his abilities in the first few Playoff Games of his life. He hit his first two NBA game-winning shots in the Playoffs during this first series against the Wizards. LeBron James averaged an unthinkable 31.4 points and 7 rebounds in the 2005-2006 season, rivaling his best production even from High School. The difference was that now, on the world stage, LeBron had again found out how to play his game and was firing on all cylinders. He was even beginning to show the world how he could step up during a Playoff environment to give his team the extra effort necessary to win that Championship some day. LeBron James was crowned the NBA's All Star Game's Most Valuable Player, and people were beginning to see his potential stretched beyond their expectations.

That season is a demonstration of how LeBron James shines when he is allowed to perform and excel within a routine. The early years for LeBron were spent seeking the kind of structure and regularity that would allow his talent to bloom into hardened skill. He thrived in the private school environment, despite being challenged by the continued attention of the national stage. Now, with Cleveland, he was allowed to stay with one team, in one environment, with one job: to win a Championship.

It's rare that a team who hasn't played together for long win the NBA National Title. No matter what kind of talent exists in individual form, the team concept of basketball and the sheer athleticism of the NBA make chemistry and collective improvisation a critical part of succeeding in the Playoffs.

In 2006-2007, Cleveland fans delighted to see that energy present on their team for the first time in close to a decade. Not only did Cleveland make it to the Playoffs for the second year in a row, but they advanced all the way to the Conference Finals, largely as a result of LeBron's exceptional play.

Picture this. You somehow managed to get a ticket to Game 5 of the Eastern Conference Finals to see LeBron James, along with Drew Gooden, Zydrunas Ilgauskas, Sasha Pavlovic and Larry Hughes take the court against the odds on favorites Pistons. The series is tied at 2 games apiece, which has stunned Pistons fans. They were expected to have moved on to the Finals by this point on the backs of star players like Chauncey Billups and Rasheed Wallace. But no, they have to get through the Cleveland Cavaliers first!

The atmosphere is thick with anticipation as the game starts, as you can see both teams vie for control of the pace of play. Members of the capacity crowd are wearing black t-shirts that say "Witness," referring to Cleveland's rise to prominence, the wearers believe completely that the Cavs are destined for greatness this year. The second half of this game saw what some people still consider LeBron's all time career best performance.

Seeing his team in need, LeBron James becomes aggressive, smart, and takes over. While you're on your feet, LeBron James goes on to score 29 of Cleveland's last 30 points. He dominates the Pistons single handedly, and scores the winning basket in the final seconds to give Cleveland a 3-2 lead in the series. In that single Playoff game, LeBron James scored 48 points.

This flash of superstardom wasn't enough to win Cleveland the title though, as they went on to be swept in their first NBA Finals ever. But LeBron James still averaged over 22 points per game in his debut to the highest level of basketball, the NBA Finals. If you were at any of those games, you probably held on to your black "Witness" shirt, with firm belief that the Cavaliers would some day reach the pinnacle of basketball greatness.

Quietly, amid all this excitement, LeBron and Savannah welcomed their second boy into the world in 2007, Bryce. Bryce joined young Lebron Jr. as a member of LeBron James' ultimate fan club.

The next year, during the NBA season from 2007-2008, the Cleveland Cavaliers again made the playoffs, but fell in the second round. This year, however, LeBron continued his personal growth on the team. He averaged 30 points per game, which earned him his first ever NBA scoring title, meaning he scored the greatest number of points of any player that year.

The 2008 Olympic games were vastly different from the 2004 games for LeBron and Team USA. This time around, in Beijing, LeBron played a major role in bringing home Gold atop a 10-0 undefeated record in the international tournament. LeBron spoke publicly about what it meant to wear a USA jersey, and how much it meant to represent the people of the United States.

LeBron James had grown from a talented High School player to a startlingly good NBA player. He appeared to be single-handedly pulling the once irrelevant Cleveland team into their current spot as perennial Playoff attendees. It seemed like it was only a matter of time before their moment in the sun would come, and Cleveland would taste its first franchise NBA Championship.

The next two consecutive seasons saw LeBron James' role on the Cleveland Cavaliers change, and grow even further. He was asked to play point guard amid injuries to the rest of the roster, which only increased his playing time and the number of touches he received on the ball. LeBron also grew into a more formidable defensive player during this period, from the 2008-2009 season to the 2009-2010 season. LeBron was named 2008-2009 Defensive Player of the Year, and was named to the NBA All-Defensive team. These additions to his play made him the league MVP in both the 2008-2009 and 2009-2010 seasons.

To understand LeBron's determination as a defensive player during these years, imagine the details of what's called a "Chase-Down Block." It's one thing to be posted up in the defensive position, with an opposing player rising to shoot right in front of you. A standard "Block" is when you, as the defender, rise to swat or impede the shot being made against you. But a "Chase-Down Block" starts on the other end of the court. Maybe your team just lost the ball in a turnover, and that opposing player is already racing down the court to score. LeBron James was able to chase that player down a record 23 times in order to block what would otherwise be an easy layup. In 2008-2009, LeBron James led his team in rebounds, points, blocks, assists and steals. It's difficult to lead your team in anything else.

Despite LeBron's incredible additions to his game from 2008-2010, Cleveland was unable to achieve the ultimate goal of a Championship.

The 2008-2009 Playoffs may have been the most heartbreaking for LeBron and Clevelanders alike. It looked like everything had finally gone the way of the Cavs. LeBron is on his game. He's been named the 2008-2009 MVP, and he's playing defense like he was born to do it. He's led the team in everything this year, including leading the team to 66 wins, nearly setting a league record for most wins in a season. Cleveland is completely unbeaten through two Playoff series, and they've fought their way to the Conference Finals against the Orlando Magic.

LeBron James somehow manages to score 49 points in this first game against the Magic. Almost 70% of the time he takes a shot, he makes it. It must have been desperately frustrating for LeBron James to feel like he was carrying the team, and yet it still wasn't enough to win that Game 1.

LeBron continued to carry the team though, because that's what he knows how to do. In Game 2, he was the player who reached down deep and found a way to score the game winning shot, leveling the series at 1-1. Somehow, Cleveland went on to lose these Conference Finals, despite LeBron scoring over 38 points per game. He had scored over 35 points per game in the Playoffs that year, but came away empty handed yet again.

Imagine playing the best basketball you've ever played, for the only NBA team you've ever played for, and you come up short again like that. For LeBron James, the only thing he's worked his entire life for is the ultimate basketball championship, and he's come so close so many times. He has taken a team from obscurity to Conference Finals, and even Finals, for the last four years. But so much has to come together to achieve Championship gold, and it wasn't yet time for one of the greatest players the NBA had ever seen. He was setting records left and right, but his only real goal was still evading him.

Chapter 6:

The Decision

It's important to see these events up until now, in order to understand what came next for LeBron James. He is from Akron, Ohio, and he's played basketball at the highest levels his entire life for Ohio teams. Now, at 26 years young, LeBron James become a free agent in the NBA. He's faced with a decision: to stay with the team that's been built around him, the hungry Cleveland Cavaliers, or look elsewhere for a chance to win a title.

Consider the Regular Seasons and the Playoffs LeBron has just been through, from his perspective. As the MVP of the league for the last two years LeBron has set defensive and offensive records for years now. He's a staple in the All Star Games. He's been on a team that, since making the Playoffs in 2005, hasn't missed a chance to go and be beaten by some new team. And each time they lose in the Playoffs, or the Conference Finals, or the Finals. LeBron seems to have an incredible individual performance each time, but still falls short of the title.

The culmination of these things was an hour long televised ESPN discussion with LeBron James called "The Decision." Over the course of this TV Special, LeBron James announced his intention to leave Cleveland for the Miami Heat of South Beach. Not only that, but LeBron James was to be joined in

Chapter 6: The Decision

Cleveland by other marquee free agents Dwayne Wade and Chris Bosh.

The move shocked and devastated the people of Cleveland. They had watched this homegrown superstar pull their basketball program out of the shadows and into the limelight. The people of Cleveland believed that a Championship was finally within reach. With LeBron, they had returned to the perennial playoff picture, and even reached the Finals for the first time in franchise history. It felt so close. And now, LeBron was ruining it.

The city of Cleveland used the word "betrayal" to describe the Decision. They felt betrayed that LeBron James was more interested in a Championship than succeeding in Cleveland, for Cleveland. What's more, LeBron had apparently conspired with the other free agents, Wade and Bosh, to build their own "super team" in South Beach. They appeared to be using the NBA to get what they wanted, a Championship, wherever it suited them best.

The Miami Heat President Pat Riley appealed to LeBron James' desire to participate in a team, instead of being forced to carry a team. LeBron was promised a role on a team that didn't involve huge net point scoring needs, but would involve more passing and strategy. The Heat intended to use LeBron within a system that didn't heap massive amounts of expectations onto him, but instead asked him to see the game and enable other players to score like he does so well.

When positioned this way, it's easy to see why LeBron James made The Decision. He was used to huge expectations, but he felt like even these historic performances weren't enough to win a championship. He needed a team behind him, and in front of him, if he were ever to realize his dream of winning a title.

LeBron was about to leave Ohio to play basketball for the first time ever, and he televised his decision nationally on ESPN like it was a special promotional video for a product. Even though the TV special produced millions of dollars for the chosen charity, the Boys and Girls Club of America, the people of Cleveland were bitter and livid. Even the Cavaliers organization was livid, having only found out about LeBron's actual choice in the minutes leading up the the airing of the show. Like it or not, LeBron James had made up his mind to join a new organization in a new state, and nothing would stop him from winning a title.

Chapter 7:

Miami

L eBron landed in Miami to a very different atmosphere. The Heat threw a welcome party at the stadium that was raucous, audacious, and extravagant. LeBron spoke to the huge crowd, who had come to celebrate the addition of these three monumental players to the team. He called the move the beginning of a dynasty, and described the team's intention to bring to Miami titles for many years to come. The rest of the league looked on with disdain at the festivities, which were a symbol to many of the collusion of these players to get what they want. This became a negative perception of LeBron, not the least of which was felt in Cleveland.

Every time LeBron played in Cleveland over the 2010-2011 season, he was booed aggressively. The sting of betrayal was deep for the people of Cleveland. But the trio of James, Wade, and Bosh proved effective from the outset of their time together. That first year in Miami, LeBron James visited the NBA Finals with his new teammates. And as predicted, it happened with a lessened scoring load from James over the regular season. He wasn't pulling as much of the load for the team. He was assisting, playing defense, and still contributing all star scoring performances.

Those first Finals for the Heat, now with LeBron, were a failed effort. LeBron James lacked the aggression and finesse often associated with his Playoff play. He was used to carrying teams, especially during these crucial moments and now the world saw a player with reduced expectations play down to those expectations. He averaged only a few points in the fourth quarters of the Finals, and the Heat lost in 6 games to Dallas.

Cleveland fans, bitter at LeBron for his perceived betrayal, rejoiced at his shortfall.

What comes next in LeBron's career is nothing short of greatness. He had let his new team down in the critical stage of their campaign, ending with a depressing loss in the Finals. His old team and his home felt betrayed by his move, and all he could do was look forward.

LeBron James, as one of the greatest players to ever play the game, is not someone to lie down and quit. He accepted blame where it was due, and he made a plan to improve. He is one of the most talented living players, yet he admitted he had room to improve within the Miami system, and he set about on an offseason training regimen to improve a specific part of his game. Within the Miami Heat, and the talented players on the team, LeBron knew that he had to become a more formidable post player. This means that as one of the largest players on the court, he had to improve his game low toward the basket, both as a target for offensive passes, and his ability to convert passes into short baskets against some of the biggest defensive centers in the world. LeBron James began to focus his game on being one of these massive post players.

He worked hard, within a very aggressive off-season routine, and when LeBron James returned for the 2011-2012 season, he appeared to many as a different player entirely. He was named MVP for the third time in his career, and the Heat again went to the Playoffs.

This was a different LeBron James from the previous year. Many observers and teammates, cited that he was humble, hungry, and motivated. Perhaps it was the engagement to his high school sweetheart, Savannah, that also served to motivate him. He scored 40 points as part of a series comeback in round two, to defeat the Pacers.

In the Conference Finals, a familiar LeBron James showed up to save the Heat from elimination. Taking the team again on his back, LeBron scored 45 points to send the series to a Game 7, which the Heat won in order to advance to the Finals. This LeBron James is the man who would buckle down to give the team the play they needed from him, even if it meant being a post player. It also meant he would step up to give them an exceptional individual performance when it was needed, like he did in these Finals, just like in past Finals for the Cavaliers.

It was during these NBA Finals, in 2011 against the Oklahoma City Thunder, that LeBron introduced himself to the world as a Champion. He rose time and time again during the series, overcoming leg cramps and spasms, to deliver crucial offense and defense for his teammates. And it was this extra effort that earned LeBron James his first ever NBA title.

Imagine being at that game, watching as LeBron James lifts the NBA Championship trophy for the first time, 8 years after entering the NBA, with a new team. Imagine the crushing weight that left his shoulders as he hoisted the golden object toward a thundering audience. LeBron James was awarded the Bill Russell NBA Finals Most Valuable player for his extreme exertion and performance during the series. The vote for this award was unanimous.

2011 was a special year for LeBron for a variety of reasons. In addition to this momentous victory, LeBron became engaged to his longtime girlfriend at the age of 27. It's incredible to imagine the life of a 27-year old basketball superstar, who has just won his first long sought world championship, also about to embark on a lifelong love. In 2012, LeBron led the Men's National Basketball team to another Gold medal in the London Olympics. This marked yet another milestone on LeBron's journey of maturation, as he had become a leader of the National team as well.

The people of Cleveland looked on as their homegrown boy raised that trophy in another town, barely two years after leaving Ohio. Imagine the competing feelings of betrayal, hatred, and pride on the part of Clevelanders for LeBron.

The 2012-2013 season would be possibly even more impressive for LeBron James, who had now found his place on his new team. He led the Heat on one of the longest winning streaks of all time, which stretched to 27 games. When Miami had finished this regular season, they had achieved a record of 66-16. For this performance, largely as a result of LeBron's superb play, he was awarded his fourth NBA MVP award.

It was no surprise then, that the Miami Heat, including LeBron James, Dwayne Wade, and Chris Bosh, would feature yet again in the NBA Finals of 2013. This would be a special series for LeBron, as it was against his very first NBA Finals opponent, the Spurs. LeBron James shattered his previous effort against the Spurs, tying an all time record for points scored in a Finals Game 7, scoring 37 points and earning him yet another Finals MVP award.

Back to back championships in Miami, in the second and third years since his departure from Cleveland. LeBron James had arrived as an All Star, and now he had the hardware to prove it. LeBron James showed no signs of stopping. He was free of the career of expectations which demanded a championship from him. He had shattered critics' voices, broadcasting their doubts that he would never fit well within a team dynamic, and that he wasn't enough to carry a team by himself to win it all. LeBron James proved in these back to back years in Miami that he could learn from his mistakes, that he had plenty left to improve in his game, and that he could still deliver the unmistakably spectacular performances when his team needed him the most. These years mark some of the greatest moments in LeBron's career as a player, since they are the first time he achieved his ultimate goal of winning a championship, and had apparently followed up on his promise to deliver a dynasty to Miami.

The next year in Miami saw yet another Finals visit, albeit an unsuccessful campaign. This team was one of only four teams in history to ever visit the NBA finals four seasons in a row. LeBron again played spectacular, averaging over 28 points during the Finals. However, his playing time was limited to due leg cramps, and ultimately the Heat were defeated, preventing a third consecutive title.

These years in Miami are an important window into LeBron James, as a player and a person. On the one hand, LeBron revealed his deep personal desire to win a Championship at any cost, by leaving his home to pursue his goal in Miami. He showed the world that he would do whatever it takes to become one of the best basketball players ever to play the game. He didn't want to be the only player carrying a team to victory, since he believed that he wouldn't be likely to succeed at the highest levels this way. LeBron James saw his plan to win a championship evaporate in front of him at a critical stage in his first Miami campaign, and admitted there was a lot more he could do to help the team win. He set aside the huge player persona after the loss of those Finals, he adopted a more modest attitude, and he set to work on improving himself as a player. He worked hard within his routine, changing the way he operated as a basketball player.

Imagine doing something your entire life, having a particular attitude every day, and realizing you need to change if you're going to move forward. On the largest stage, LeBron James came to that realization and became a monumental post-player. He changed the way he thought and played in order to serve his team and his organization, above himself. This can be considered one of the major maturing moments in LeBron James' career, when he learned to put the team above himself. For his immense personal growth and effort, he was rewarded by being able to lift a Championship Trophy in back to back seasons with Miami. He was recognized at the MVP of both of those Finals. These are testaments to his growth and his journey, from a young basketball player to a mature superstar.

Chapter 8:

The Return

In the summer of 2014, LeBron James elected to leave Miami and the Heat team he had been to four consecutive Finals with. This time, LeBron James did not hold a special televised event to tell the people of Cleveland he would be returning to them. Some observers speculate that LeBron wasn't sure the reaction would be positive, and this worry motivated his decision to write a short essay for Sports Illustrated about his return to Cleveland.

However, he had nothing to worry about. In a now famous reception, the people of Cleveland and Ohio welcomed LeBron James back home with a sweeping parade. They accepted him back with open arms, as the prodigal son of Ohio basketball. So what caused LeBron to leave such a successful Miami team, with whom he had achieved two titles? LeBron described his readiness to be home, to be among the people and communities he had grown up with and in. He felt connected to the city of Cleveland, and saw himself raising his young family there, rather than in Miami.

There would even be some changes to the team that would support LeBron's return. Just as in Miami, there would be a pair of additional stars to support his talent and relieve the scoring burden a bit. Kevin Love and Kyrie Irving were set to compliment LeBron as he rejoined his home franchise of the Cleveland Cavaliers.

Cleveland fans, having watched LeBron's thunderous success in Miami, began to allow themselves to believe once again that a Championship would come to their fair city. Excitement began to build as LeBron promised a new era of Cleveland basketball.

He was right, of course. In his first season back in Cleveland, LeBron James again visited the Finals. This was his fifth consecutive Finals trip, unheard of in the NBA since the 60s. LeBron James revived his famous Finals performances, delivering an average of over 35 points per game in the championship rounds. Despite eventually losing in this first trip to the Finals after being back in Cleveland, LeBron played well enough to be considered a candidate for MVP of the Finals. The Cleveland Cavaliers had their star back, and he was as good as ever.

LeBron had learned to be an excellent defensive player during his time in Miami, and Cleveland was now benefiting from his experience and work. LeBron continued to present the same domination of the paint that he had learned in Miami. He had grown from an offensive-minded explosive player into a more strategic player, more careful and calculating in the way that he used his prominent bulk.

2014 also saw the arrival of Zhuri James, Lebron's youngest of three children, into the world. Zhuri is a favorite at press conferences, where she looks straight at the cameras.

The 2015-2016 season meant everything for Cleveland Cavaliers fans. Despite some controversy, like the loss of their head coach midway through the season, the Cavaliers had found magic on the court. Cleveland won 57 games, and went to the Finals once again (that's LeBron's sixth consecutive trip to the Finals, in case you're still counting).

The Cleveland Cavaliers, under the leadership of their champion, LeBron, and his cast of talented teammates, advanced to the Finals to face the formidable Golden State Warriors, who had just had a record setting year. The Warriors had won a stunning 73 games during the season. It looked like the Warriors would blow right past the Cavaliers as well, by recording two huge victories in games 1 and 2. The Warriors beat the Cavaliers 104-89 and 110-77 in these two initial games, making it look like once again the Cavaliers would be robbed of a title.

With a LeBron James 32 point performance in Game 3, the Cavaliers fought back to take a win from the Warriors.

A tough Game 4 saw a Cleveland loss of only 108-97. They were keeping it close, but were now facing a 3-1 series deficit, and the Cleveland Cavaliers were fighting for survival. A single loss would mean the end of yet another season, and yet another unsuccessful Finals. The Golden State Warriors were all but secured as the 2015-2016 NBA Champions. The futile hopes of the people of Ohio hung in the balance, as the world waited to see what LeBron James and the Cavaliers would be able to do, if anything. No team had ever successfully come back from a 3-1 deficit in the NBA finals before.

The remaining games of these Finals would have been incredible to attend. LeBron James found a level of play never before considered possible. His defense and offense were incredible, and he was able to score 41 points in both games 5 and 6. Irving also scored 41 points in Game 5, and the Cleveland Cavaliers took Game 5 from the Warriors with a score of 112-97. The Cavaliers won to stay alive yet again in Game 6 with a score of 115-101. In this game, LeBron scored 18 straight points late in the game to surge Cleveland ahead.

With massive performances from LeBron, Irving, and Kevin Love, the Cleveland Cavaliers had done the impossible to force a Game 7 in the NBA Final against one of the best Warriors teams to take the court. Stephen Curry, the consistent leader of the Warriors, had to be shut down if the Cavaliers had a chance. Curry had been instrumental in getting the Warriors to their record setting season. Not only that, but LeBron would have to show up with his best offensive self if the Cavaliers were to compete with the 100 plus point games the Warriors had been racking up against Cleveland.

In Game 7 of the 2015-2016 NBA Finals, LeBron James did just that. He achieved what is known as a triple-double. That means he tallied double-digit statistics in scoring, rebounding, and assists in the final game of the series. LeBron completed many triple-doubles over the course of his career, but this one in Game 7 was exactly the kind of clutch performance expected of a superstar. Cleveland pulled together to not only stave off elimination after falling to a 3-1 deficit in the series, they found a way to win in Game 7.

It was with this win that LeBron James brought the first professional championship to the city of Cleveland in over 50 years. He had worked his entire career to create a championship team in Cleveland, and in 2016, it finally happened.

The celebration was enormous. The City of Cleveland went crazy. LeBron James had returned from Miami to lead the Cavaliers to the victory that millions of people had waited for for over 10 years, since LeBron was first drafted as a Rookie to

Cleveland in 2003. He had abandoned the city to win two championships in Miami, visiting the Finals each year of his absence. Now he had decided to return home to raise his family and bring a Championship to his hometown. The city of Cleveland has experienced sporting heartbreaks for the last 50 years, and many people thought that the departure of LeBron James was yet another in the streak. His decision to move to Miami would not be the end of Cleveland basketball, however, as he and the talented team had proven in this pivotal Final.

After numerous failed trips to the Finals with Cleveland, LeBron finally had the team he needed to win. They beat one of the most talented overall squads in the 2015-2016 Warriors with a spectacular once-in-a-lifetime come from behind victory in the last game, as part of a huge come from behind surge in what many thought was a lost series.

What LeBron James has done for the hopes and dreams of the City of Cleveland will forever be remembered, both as a player and a hometown hero. He is an inspiration to kids all over the world, as someone who came from challenging circumstances, and with motivation and hard work won the hearts and minds of people all over the world, not to mention several titles.

Chapter 9:

Challenges and Criticism

L eBron James has led a life almost entirely in the public eye. As such, he has faced many challenges over the course of his career, for which he has received public scrutiny and criticism.

Early on, as LeBron finished High School, there were a pair of incidents involving accepting gifts or compensation in exchange for his athletic achievement. The first incident had to do with accepting sports memorabilia in exchange for posing for pictures. This was the incident he was suspended for. Another incident saw his mother purchase him a Hummer, using a line of credit established from his future professional income. He was not punished for this, since the gift did not come from a recruiter or a potential sponsor, but as a gift from his family. This still brought negative attention to his life as a young man.

That attention became difficult to deal with, and during his senior year of High School LeBron was found to be using marijuana to cope. The usage wasn't serious or pervasive, and this relatively minor scandal blew over quickly for the young James.

Chapter 9: Challenges and Criticism

Once LeBron got his start in the NBA, he was also placed on the US National Team, and got his first opportunity to play in the Olympics in Greece. However, he did not play very much, primarily because his coaching staff and team were not pleased with his attitude. This was compounded when James was accused of mistreating the support staff during the FIBA international tournament, for which he received negative media attention during the games. In order to play in the subsequent Beijing Olympics with the National Team, LeBron James was asked to improve his attitude, which he did. This type of scandal would taint LeBron's public image for a time, portraying him as a slightly conceited player.

LeBron didn't improve his public image following the 2008 Finals with Cleveland. Recall that during these Finals, LeBron outperformed his teammates by leaps and bounds, but Cleveland still wasn't able to convert the effort into the city's first title. LeBron, frustrated, left after the final buzzer without shaking any hands. This act was viewed as being very unsportsmanlike, and LeBron received criticism for his actions.

As a young player, LeBron James faced criticism for being a primarily offensive player, without many redeeming defensive skills. He was known for his explosive shot and his forward power, his eye for passing and game control, but when it came time for defense, LeBron was viewed as weak.

It was only in the later years of his career, especially after losing that first Final in Miami, that LeBron is considered to have risen as a truly great defensive player. It was in the years that followed that LeBron won defensive awards, was placed on the NBA All-Defense team, and started accumulating large block statistics.

Chapter 10:

Charity

As one of the highest paid sporting figures in the world, and the highest paid basketball player, LeBron James has been generous in his wealth. He recently donated money to renovate the gymnasium of St. Vincent-St. Mary's High School, his alma mater.

His foundation regularly raises money via a bike-a-thon, and one of his primary recipients of charitable giving is the Boys and Girls Club of America. The LeBron James Foundation seeks to help single mothers, like LeBron's mother and Foundation partner Gloria, who worked so hard to give LeBron the life she knew he deserved. LeBron donated the proceeds of his televised program "The Decision" to the Boys and Girls Club of America when he left Cleveland in 2011.

LeBron and his mother Gloria have formed a powerful partnership that has inspired the LeBron James Foundation to act on behalf of single mothers everywhere. LeBron has clearly come to have a deep respect for the women who raise families by themselves, and the children from these families. Together, LeBron and Gloria seek to inspire and support these families around the world.

Chapter 11:

Sponsors

LeBron was the target of large sponsors from an early age. In High School at St. Vincent-St. Mary's, he was unable to accept any sponsorship deals. But after signing with the NBA, LeBron became eligible to sign with sponsors and participate in his own contracts with them. The first and largest of these sponsors was Nike, who paid him upwards of 90 million dollars. As part of the Nike deal, LeBron James has been part of the Nike line of LeBron shoes now for more than ten years. These shoes are very popular, making the deal a profitable one for both Nike and LeBron. LeBron's contract for Nike is for life, an astounding commitment for an athlete and a sponsor to make to each other. So far, the deal has been more than agreeable.

The initial deal was valued at 90 million dollars, now some observers speculate it may be worth as much as one billion with the incentives available for sales.

Other notable sponsorships include his stake in the English Premier League, his partnership with Coca Cola (more recently famous as a face of Sprite), and his stake in Beats electronics.

Chapter 11: Sponsors

LeBron has long been one of the highest paid basketball players, and became the highest paid player in the world in 2013, making over 56 million dollars.

Chapter 12:

What's Next for LeBron

Now 32 years old, LeBron James still has a career to look forward to with the Cleveland Cavaliers. He signed a 3 year, 100-million-dollar extension in August of 2016 that will keep him in Cleveland, and also continue to make him the highest paid basketball player in the league.

Who knows just how many more years LeBron will spend in the league, and how many more championships he will attain. It remains purely up to speculation, but the odds are that more championship success will be coming his way yet. Just where he will end up in the 'greatest of all time' discussion remains to be seen, but many speculate that he has a chance of outranking Michael Jordan when it's all said and done.

There is another LeBron James making news, and that's Junior. LeBron's oldest son is 11, and he's starting to make some of the same waves that his dad did at his age. He's superbly talented, and is reportedly being recruited already by colleges. Soon the media will be following him as closely as they did his father, and he'll have the best possible father to help him with the pressure of media coverage. One of LeBron's oldest and most consistent challenges has been the expectations leveled against him by the media, scouts, and from around the league. He has now set the bar very high for young LeBron James Junior, who seems to be stepping up to the plate, much as his father did. Could young LeBron outpace the senior LeBron? Only time will tell.

LeBron James and his family will be in Cleveland for the foreseeable future, and the basketball gifts of the father may be passed down to future generations for Clevelanders to look forward to.

Conclusion

Thanks again for taking the time to read this book! You should now have a good understanding of LeBron James and his inspiring life!

If you enjoyed this book, please take the time to leave me a review on Amazon. I appreciate your honest feedback, and it really helps me to continue producing high quality books.